Junior Maths

Book 2

Answer Book

GALORE PARK

Junior Maths

Book 2

Answer Book

David Hillard

Series Editor: Louise Martine

www.galorepark.co.uk

Published by Galore Park Publishing Ltd
338 Euston Road, London NW1 3BH

www.galorepark.co.uk

Text copyright © David Hillard 2008
Illustrations copyright © Galore Park 2008

The right of David Hillard to be identified as the author of this Work has been
asserted by him in accordance with sections 77 and 78 of the Copyright,
Designs and Patents Act 1988.

Typography and layout by Typetechnique, London W1
Technical drawings by Simon Tegg and Ian Moores

Printed and bound by CPI Group (UK) Ltd, Croydon, CR0 4YY

ISBN: 978 1 905735 24 2

First published 2008, reprinted 2009, 2011, 2012, 2013, 2015

The textbook to accompany these answers is available from www.galorepark.co.uk

Details of other Galore Park publications are available at www.galorepark.co.uk

ISEB Revision Guides, publications and examination papers may also be obtained
from Galore Park.

Preface

This book provides a complete set of answers to *Junior Maths Book 2* (ISBN: 978 1 905735 23 5).

Contents

Chapter 1: Place value

Exercise 1.1: Writing numbers

1. (a) Sixty-seven
    (b) Eighty
    (c) Three hundred and sixty-one
    (d) Four hundred and fifty
    (e) Seven hundred and two
    (f) Eight hundred and sixty-six

2. (a) 300
    (b) 0
    (c) 30
    (d) 6
    (e) 80
    (f) 7

3. (a) 400
    (b) 73
    (c) 149
    (d) 650
    (e) 264
    (f) 340

Exercise 1.2: Place value and larger numbers

1. 4000
2. 200 000
3. 10 000
4. 2000
5. 700
6. 30
7. 100 000
8. 9
9. 70 000
10. 400
11. 6
12. 20 000
13. 50
14. 3000
15. 100 000

Exercise 1.3: Writing larger numbers in words

1. Four thousand, one hundred and twenty-five
2. One thousand, seven hundred and thirty-two
3. Five thousand, nine hundred and eighty-one
4. Seven thousand, one hundred and thirty-eight
5. Three thousand, six hundred and forty
6. Six thousand and twenty-seven
7. One thousand, five hundred
8. Two thousand, five hundred and ninety-eight
9. Five thousand and fifty
10. Eight thousand and five
11. Nineteen thousand, two hundred and forty-six
12. Ten thousand, seven hundred

13. Fifty-seven thousand, two hundred and fourteen
14. Eighty-four thousand, three hundred and eighty-six
15. Sixty-two thousand, three hundred and seventy-two
16. Thirty-two thousand, one hundred and eight
17. Fifty-one thousand, two hundred and seventy-five
18. Twelve thousand, six hundred
19. Seventy-five thousand
20. Forty-three thousand and ten
21. One hundred and seventy-two thousand, nine hundred and thirty-four
22. One hundred and twenty-four thousand, seven hundred and twelve
23. Seven hundred and twenty-eight thousand, five hundred and thirty-six
24. Two hundred and ninety-four thousand, three hundred and seventy-one
25. Nine hundred and twenty thousand, three hundred and twenty-one
26. Eight hundred and forty-two thousand, four hundred and ninety-seven
27. One hundred and sixty-two thousand, five hundred and thirty-four
28. Two hundred and forty-three thousand and twenty
29. Two hundred thousand, one hundred and sixty
30. One hundred and one thousand and ten

Exercise 1.4: Writing larger numbers in figures

1.	3649	11.	18 348	21.	226 527
2.	8320	12.	27 184	22.	625 213
3.	1202	13.	59 642	23.	112 868
4.	5857	14.	73 901	24.	700 000
5.	7000	15.	99 919	25.	420 600
6.	3105	16.	40 000	26.	807 090
7.	9890	17.	30 400	27.	324 206
8.	3501	18.	53 060	28.	208 300
9.	8600	19.	81 005	29.	500 050
10.	3003	20.	19 201	30.	660 006

Exercise 1.5: Ordering numbers

1. (a) 3841   974   17
   (b) 2316   1483   627
   (c) 7300   5142   4901

(d) 8635	8569	7432		
(e) 5839	5493	5273		
(f) 6733	6732	6730		
(g) 7165	6715	5761	1567	
(h) 8643	8634	3486	3468	
(i) 20 873	18 492	9479		
(j) 59 723	41 685	40 175		
(k) 39 568	38 700	37 392		
(l) 73 291	73 146	73 037		
(m) 84 269	84 264	84 263		
(n) 34 512	34 125	12 543	12 345	
(o) 26 841	26 481	26 184	26 148	
(p) 86 092	86 054	86 045	86 029	
(q) 129 308	120 987	12 642		
(r) 863 517	743 289	356 284		
(s) 165 895	165 859	165 589		
(t) 683 192	672 135	652 072		
(u) 342 168	341 168	332 168	323 168	
(v) 312 654	231 546	132 465	123 456	
(w) 109 386	109 385	109 384	109 380	
(x) 143 209	42 185	27 486	4819	4637
(y) 87 348	87 329	87 175	87 142	87 064
(z) 643 621	643 612	643 216	643 162	643 126

2.

(a) 37	486	1029		
(b) 389	954	1528		
(c) 2816	3217	4210		
(d) 7019	7842	7916		
(e) 4828	4837	4896		
(f) 2819	2945	2948		
(g) 1480	1486	1489	1490	
(h) 2963	3629	3692	9236	
(i) 9898	26 217	31 400		
(j) 38 172	43 219	43 506		
(k) 48 208	48 219	48 223		
(l) 34 168	34 618	34 816		
(m) 89 563	89 564	89 567		
(n) 23 186	23 816	59 234	59 324	

(o) 14 723	14 732	14 733	14 734	
(p) 23 793	24 285	26 603	27 821	
(q) 1038	10 386	103 860		
(r) 349 862	421 963	583 206		
(s) 518 729	562 987	586 175		
(t) 374 192	374 291	374 921		
(u) 172 486	173 841	174 831	178 341	
(v) 310 567	310 576	310 675	310 765	
(w) 123 456	234 561	435 162	561 234	
(x) 2943	83 251	83 260	106 300	113 250
(y) 72 400	72 411	72 417	72 471	72 477
(z) 52 014	52 104	52 140	52 410	521 004

Exercise 1.6: Summary exercise

1. (a) 8642
    (b) 2468

    (c)
2468	4268	6248	8246
2486	4286	6284	8264
2648	4628	6824	8426
2684	4682	6842	8462
2864	4862	6482	8624
2846	4826	6428	8642

2. (a) Twenty-four thousand, three hundred and ten
    (b) 302 016

3. (a) 200   (b) 200 000   (c) 70 000   (d) 8000

4. (a) 421 500   421 000   42 199
    (b) 43 100   43 000   34 160
    (c) 109 347   109 345   109 342   109 340

5. (a) 327   783   1891
    (b) 4823   4832   9167   9176
    (c) 127 378   127 387   127 783   127 873

End of chapter activity: Binary arithmetic

1. 2
2. 3
3. 4
4. 7
5. 10

6. 13
7. 14
8. 16
9. 21
10. 27

Chapter 2: Counting

Exercise 2.1: Counting in tens

1.
(a) 72	82	92	102	112	122	132
(b) 160	170	180	190	200	210	220
(c) 285	295	305	315	325	335	345
(d) 1640	1650	1660	1670	1680	1690	1700
(e) 3600	3610	3620	3630	3640	3650	3660
(f) 2215	2225	2235	2245	2255	2265	2275

2.
(a) 94	(c) 227	(e) 1881
(b) 133	(d) 324	(f) 1010

3.
(a) 92	82	72	62	52	42	32
(b) 130	120	110	100	90	80	70
(c) 217	207	197	187	177	167	157
(d) 1030	1020	1010	1000	990	980	970
(e) 2570	2560	2550	2540	2530	2520	2510
(f) 3425	3415	3405	3395	3385	3375	3365
(g) 6700	6690	6680	6670	6660	6650	6640
(h) 5105	5095	5085	5075	5065	5055	5045

4.
(a) 21	(c) 286	(e) 5257
(b) 53	(d) 3679	(f) 4580

Exercise 2.2: Counting in hundreds

1.
(a) 850	950	1050	1150	1250	1350	1450
(b) 1700	1800	1900	2000	2100	2200	2300
(c) 2870	2970	3070	3170	3270	3370	3470
(d) 3694	3794	3894	3994	4094	4194	4294
(e) 9860	9960	10 060	10 160	10 260	10 360	10 460
(f) 8292	8392	8492	8592	8692	8792	8892

2.
(a) 859	(c) 2300	(e) 8095
(b) 1443	(d) 3041	(f) 5282

3.
(a)	1200	1100	1000	900	800	700	600
(b)	3700	3600	3500	3400	3300	3200	3100
(c)	4100	4000	3900	3800	3700	3600	3500
(d)	2550	2450	2350	2250	2150	2050	1950
(e)	10 300	10 200	10 100	10 000	9900	9800	9700
(f)	1090	990	890	790	690	590	490

4.
(a) 478　　　(c) 1800　　　(e) 11 500
(b) 400　　　(d) 2950　　　(f) 10 100

Exercise 2.3: Counting in thousands

1.
(a)	7000	8000	9000	10 000	11 000	12 000	13 000
(b)	14 700	15 700	16 700	17 700	18 700	19 700	20 700
(c)	96 200	97 200	98 200	99 200	100 200	101 200	102 200
(d)	346 000	347 000	348 000	349 000	350 000	351 000	352 000
(e)	500 000	501 000	502 000	503 000	504 000	505 000	506 000
(f)	800 000	801 000	802 000	803 000	804 000	805 000	806 000

2.
(a) 9456　　　(c) 15 700　　　(e) 43 230
(b) 13 870　　(d) 59 580　　　(f) 46 500

3.
(a)	9000	8000	7000	6000	5000	4000	3000
(b)	27 000	26 000	25 000	24 000	23 000	22 000	21 000
(c)	81 500	80 500	79 500	78 500	77 500	76 500	75 500
(d)	100 000	99 000	98 000	97 000	96 000	95 000	94 000
(e)	810 000	809 000	808 000	807 000	806 000	805 000	804 000
(f)	30 000	29 000	28 000	27 000	26 000	25 000	24 000

4.
(a) 2650　　　(c) 14 900　　　(e) 81 000
(b) 4350　　　(d) 37 000　　　(f) 960

Exercise 2.4: Summary exercise

1. 380
2. 527
3. 603
4. 1328
5. 3005

6. 410
7. 160
8. 330
9. 4180
10. 4920

11. 710
12. 1180
13. 1450
14. 1950
15. 5100

16. 250
17. 900
18. 1650
19. 42 900
20. 60 100

21. 9400
22. 11 070
23. 22 000
24. 32 500
25. 155 000

26. 6500
27. 3600
28. 13 000
29. 36 400
30. 128 000

End of chapter activity: More binary arithmetic

1. 101
2. 1010
3. 1111
4. 11000
5. 100011

6. 101011
7. 111111
8. 1000110
9. 1010101
10. 1100100

Chapter 3: Addition

Exercise 3.1: Addition

1.	1100	6.	6800
2.	1400	7.	8500
3.	6000	8.	4200
4.	16 000	9.	8500
5.	7900	10.	12 900

11.	15 400	16.	4970
12.	11 400	17.	6880
13.	15 100	18.	8000
14.	13 000	19.	9100
15.	12 700	20.	5630

21.	8970	26.	17 010
22.	6460	27.	18 600
23.	8760	28.	14 050
24.	13 740	29.	10 450
25.	11 930	30.	14 250

31.	1402	36.	2598
32.	924	37.	3010
33.	1215	38.	7230
34.	1812	39.	9000
35.	620	40.	20 000

Exercise 3.2: Adding larger numbers

1.	598	6.	556
2.	478	7.	901
3.	187	8.	933
4.	592	9.	868
5.	768	10.	735

11.	833	16.	521
12.	1344	17.	404
13.	1302	18.	1240
14.	1000	19.	1233
15.	1243	20.	1194
21.	1113	26.	693
22.	1325	27.	831
23.	1412	28.	2124
24.	1223	29.	2279
25.	1080	30.	651
31.	559	34.	347
32.	378	35.	1839
33.	1488		

Exercise 3.3: Problem solving

1. 263 animals
2. 183 miles
3. 2642 books
4. 1852 (early 1853 is also possible)
5. 2274 runs
6. 1007 people
7. 83 items
8. 130 toy cars
9. 1138 people
10. 78 227 people

Exercise 3.4: Summary exercise

1. (a) 1200
   (b) 780
   (c) 1610
   (d) 9500
   (e) 7000
   (f) 6400
   (g) 7990
   (h) 760
   (i) 885
   (j) 3620

2. (a) 589
   (b) 563
   (c) 1370
   (d) 746
   (e) 624
   (f) 1403
   (g) 1640
   (h) 1643
   (i) 852
   (j) 1225

End of chapter activity: Magic squares

2	7	6
9	5	1
4	3	8

Each vertical, horizontal or diagonal line has a total of 15, which is three times the number in the centre.

For those lines which pass through the centre, the numbers either side of 5 need to be 5 +/– the same difference, to give a total of 15.

Using only the numbers 1 to 9, the four lines with 5 at the centre must be:

    1   5   9

    2   5   8

    3   5   7

    4   5   6

These lines can be arranged in different ways. Remember that the four outer lines must also add up to 15. For example:

8	3	4
1	5	9
6	7	2

4	3	8
9	5	1
2	7	6

8	1	6
3	5	7
4	9	2

Chapter 4: Subtraction

Exercise 4.1: Subtraction by complementary addition

1.	533		6.	115
2.	356		7.	453
3.	233		8.	264
4.	364		9.	617
5.	782		10.	513

11.	212		16.	1933
12.	383		17.	2977
13.	188		18.	7413
14.	679		19.	4460
15.	462		20.	7580

21.	5630		26.	3760
22.	3375		27.	4328
23.	737		28.	6840
24.	3914		29.	1585
25.	7702		30.	4186

Exercise 4.2: Subtraction by compensation

1.	417		6.	554
2.	274		7.	166
3.	673		8.	413
4.	257		9.	145
5.	561		10.	467

11.	212		16.	951
12.	275		17.	3922
13.	267		18.	3468
14.	274		19.	6560
15.	182		20.	1850

21. 5330
22. 6433
23. 7848
24. 5876
25. 1228

26. 2520
27. 1280
28. 2840
29. 4775
30. 2537

Exercise 4.3: Subtraction by decomposition or the formal method

1. 38
2. 56
3. 355
4. 73
5. 669

6. 667
7. 377
8. 137
9. 457
10. 177

11. 168
12. 338
13. 149
14. 368
15. 276

16. 59
17. 187
18. 62
19. 227
20. 273

21. 218
22. 319
23. 555
24. 2568
25. 1723

26. 2782
27. 6547
28. 1487
29. 2907
30. 2508

31. 517
32. 4036
33. 3254
34. 186
35. 5378

Exercise 4.4: Problem solving

1. 48 plain biscuits
2. 39 miles
3. 145
4. 503 pages
5. 52 years old

6. 1758
7. 857 seats
8. 85 points
9. 3552 miles
10. 12 941 people

Exercise 4.5: Summary exercise

1.	14		6.	321
2.	44		7.	577
3.	5		8.	313
4.	107		9.	1995
5.	106		10.	4750
11.	263		16.	538
12.	346		17.	1778
13.	277		18.	1827
14.	566		19.	4595
15.	467		20.	3255
21.	237		26.	3895
22.	576		27.	278
23.	680		28.	575
24.	166		29.	704
25.	18		30.	4517

End of chapter activity: Magic squares revisited

(a)

9	2	7
4	6	8
5	10	3

(b)

10	3	8
5	7	9
6	11	4

(c)

11	4	9
6	8	10
7	12	5

(d)

12	5	10
7	9	11
8	13	6

15	8	13
10	12	14
11	16	9

Patterns of magic squares

Each line totals three times the number in the centre.

The difference between the number in the centre and the numbers on either side of it is the same. For example, in the magic square above, the top left to bottom right diagonal has a centre of 12 and the difference either side is 3.

12 + 3 = 15

12 − 3 = 9

(a) Total is 6 x 3 = 18

5	6	7	(−/+1)
4	6	8	(−/+2)
3	6	9	(−/+3)
2	6	10	(−/+4)

(b) Total is 7 x 3 = 21

6	7	8	(−/+1)
5	7	9	(−/+2)
4	7	10	(−/+3)
3	7	11	(−/+4)

(c) Total is 8 x 3 = 24

7	8	9	(−/+1)
6	8	10	(−/+2)
5	8	11	(−/+3)
4	8	12	(−/+4)

(d) Total is 9 x 3 = 27

8	9	10	(−/+1)
7	9	11	(−/+2)
6	9	12	(−/+3)
5	9	13	(−/+4)

The numbers above can be written in this order:
- diagonally, from bottom left to top right
- across the middle from left to right
- diagonally, from bottom right to top left
- down the middle from top to bottom

Chapter 5: Addition and subtraction

Exercise 5.1: Addition and subtraction

1. 92
2. 38
3. 136
4. 98
5. 50

6. 12
7. 89
8. 47
9. 109
10. 179

11. 217
12. 536
13. 258
14. 531
15. 184

16. 1450
17. 583
18. 2936
19. 4523
20. 1081

Exercise 5.2: Inverses

1. 15
2. 15
3. 6
4. 9
5. 42

6. 18
7. 18
8. 42
9. 52
10. 52

11. 122
12. 95
13. 150
14. 272
15. 206

16. 203
17. 450
18. 300
19. 270
20. 100

Exercise 5.3: Problem solving

1. 13 children
2. 117 tins
3. 33 exercise books
4. (a) No   (b) 13 tickets short
5. 192 pints

6. 82 marbles
7. 82 marks
8. 1072 passengers
9. 66%
10. No.

Exercise 5.4: Summary exercise

1. (a) 58
   (b) 24
   (c) 100
   (d) 37

2. (a) 107
   (b) 67
   (c) 225
   (d) 65
   (e) 48
   (f) 68
   (g) 75
   (h) 37
   (i) 90
   (j) 10

End of chapter activity: A magic number

The answer will always be the same, i.e. 1089

Chapter 6: Multiplication

Exercise 6.1: Multiples

1. 3
2. 6
3. 9
4. 2
5. 4
6. 8
7. 12
8. 6
9. 11
10. 5
11. 8
12. 9
13. 5 also 25
14. 5 also 15
15. 10 also 20

Exercise 6.2: Tables

1. 24
2. 35
3. 99
4. 48
5. 54
6. 14
7. 121
8. 40
9. 36
10. 96

11. 49
12. 81
13. 110
14. 48
15. 84
16. 64
17. 77
18. 72
19. 63
20. 88

21. 108
22. 42
23. 32
24. 132
25. 45
26. 24
27. 24
28. 144
29. 72
30. 33

Exercise 6.3: Multiples of 10, 100 and 1000

1. 50
2. 1350
3. 830
4. 40 000
5. 3100
6. 81 900
7. 500 000
8. 7500
9. 345 000
10. 500

11.	25 000	**16.**	5 000 000
12.	1 780 000	**17.**	700 000
13.	20 000 000	**18.**	6 575 000
14.	382 000	**19.**	60 000
15.	8000	**20.**	1 000 000

Exercise 6.4: Square numbers

1. 1, 4, 9, 16, 25, 36, 49, 64, 81, 100

2. A square number is the result of multiplying a number by itself

Exercise 6.5: Multiplication by partition

1.	76	**6.**	518
2.	147	**7.**	224
3.	344	**8.**	153
4.	455	**9.**	567
5.	390	**10.**	228
11.	354	**16.**	776
12.	324	**17.**	249
13.	301	**18.**	243
14.	174	**19.**	469
15.	355	**20.**	216

Exercise 6.6: The formal method of multiplication (1)

1.	168	**5.**	544	**9.**	388
2.	235	**6.**	156	**10.**	114
3.	158	**7.**	342	**11.**	81
4.	112	**8.**	664	**12.**	252

Exercise 6.7: The formal method of multiplication (2)

1.	174	11.	329
2.	138	12.	549
3.	390	13.	336
4.	520	14.	375
5.	148	15.	196
6.	312	16.	306
7.	186	17.	92
8.	567	18.	120
9.	126	19.	413
10.	252	20.	114

Exercise 6.8: Further multiplication

1.	534	6.	708
2.	1088	7.	5698
3.	2145	8.	2916
4.	4452	9.	1312
5.	1332	10.	2550
11.	3412	16.	5760
12.	2187	17.	3663
13.	2625	18.	4284
14.	2955	19.	2508
15.	1968	20.	4545

Exercise 6.9: Problem solving

1.	288 tennis balls	6.	720 screws
2.	168 notebooks	7.	555 pencils
3.	324 eggs	8.	496 tyres
4.	384 cans	9.	1435 kg
5.	300 stamps	10.	585 km

Exercise 6.10: Summary exercise

1. (a) 28
    (b) 27
    (c) 66
    (d) 60
    (e) 56

    (f) 36
    (g) 44
    (h) 21
    (i) 100
    (j) 1, 4, 9, 16, 25, 36, 49

2. (a) 870
    (b) 2 396 000
    (c) 800
    (d) 45 000
    (e) 56 700

    (f) 10 000
    (g) 69 000
    (h) 650 000
    (i) 4000
    (j) 75 000 000

3. (a) 148
    (b) 104
    (c) 480
    (d) 120
    (e) 402

    (f) 255
    (g) 273
    (h) 378
    (i) 424
    (j) 558

    (k) 224
    (l) 588
    (m) 234
    (n) 477
    (o) 430

    (p) 1872
    (q) 314
    (r) 2492
    (s) 1820
    (t) 945

End of chapter activity: Another way to multiply

1.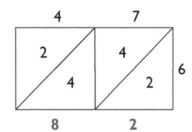

2.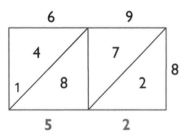

3.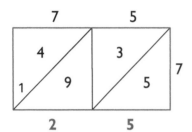

4.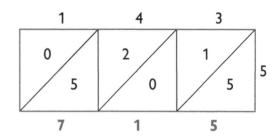

5.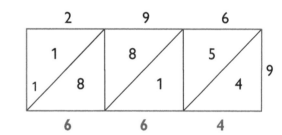

6.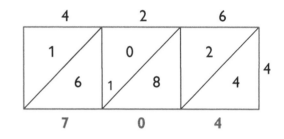

Chapter 7: Division

Exercise 7.1: Easy division

1. (a) 2
    (b) 3
    (c) 3
    (d) 3
    (e) 5

    (f) 10
    (g) 8
    (h) 5
    (i) 8
    (j) 6

2. (a) 4
    (b) 6
    (c) 8
    (d) 10
    (e) 4

    (f) 8
    (g) 7
    (h) 9
    (i) 6
    (j) 12

3. (a) 9
    (b) 11
    (c) 9
    (d) 12
    (e) 12

4. (a) 2
    (b) 4
    (c) 5
    (d) 2
    (e) 7

    (f) 5
    (g) 7
    (h) 3
    (i) 5
    (j) 2

5. (a) 5 r4
    (b) 2 r6
    (c) 9 r2
    (d) 10 r4
    (e) 11 r1

    (f) 3 r3
    (g) 2 r8
    (h) 3 r6
    (i) 2 r6
    (j) 4 r2

Exercise 7.2: Division by 10, 100 and 1000

1. 8
2. 50
3. 42
4. 430
5. 868

6. 4
7. 19
8. 547
9. 400
10. 9000

11. 5
12. 96
13. 482
14. 320
15. 900

16. 30
17. 8
18. 62
19. 450
20. 610

Exercise 7.3: Informal division

1. 16
2. 15
3. 14
4. 17
5. 16

6. 14
7. 29
8. 38
9. 14
10. 18

11. 63
12. 43
13. 37
14. 25
15. 18

16. 19
17. 17
18. 14
19. 17
20. 15

Exercise 7.4: The formal method of division

1. 37
2. 28
3. 23
4. 13

5. 14
6. 13
7. 29
8. 14

9. 17
10. 54

11. 52
12. 34
13. 27
14. 23

15. 24
16. 15
17. 14
18. 32

19. 29
20. 23

21. 268	**25.** 159	**29.** 187
22. 247	**26.** 123	**30.** 287
23. 197	**27.** 114	
24. 115	**28.** 198	

31. 88	**35.** 57	**39.** 60
32. 52	**36.** 75	**40.** 208
33. 98	**37.** 37	
34. 63	**38.** 47	

Exercise 7.5: Checking your answers

1. (a) 36
(b) 36
(c) 4
(d) 9

2. (a) 8
(b) 8
(c) 48

3. (a) 3
(b) 3
(c) 30

4. (a) 40
(b) 5

5. 5
6. 21
7. 6
8. 80
9. 5
10. 4
11. 48
12. 64

13. (a) ✓
(b) ✗
(c) ✓
(d) ✓
(e) ✗
(f) ✓
(g) ✗
(h) ✓
(i) ✓
(j) ✗

(k) ✓
(l) ✗
(m) ✓
(n) ✓
(o) ✗
(p) ✓
(q) ✗
(r) ✗
(s) ✓
(t) ✗

Exercise 7.6: Problem solving

1. 6 toffees
2. 14 boxes
3. 18 cherries
4. 3 taxis
5. 36 daffodils

6. 16 pencils
7. 50 boxes
8. 96 points
9. £225
10. 14 piles

Exercise 7.7: Summary exercise

1. (a) 7
   (b) 5
   (c) 9

   (d) 10
   (e) 5
   (f) 7

2. (a) 12
   (b) 160
   (c) 4

   (d) 35
   (e) 800

3. (a) ✗
   (b) ✓

4. (a) 14
   (b) 29
   (c) 13
   (d) 53
   (e) 64

   (f) 293
   (g) 139
   (h) 43
   (i) 102
   (j) 140

End of chapter activity: Yet another way to multiply

1.

1	2	x		2	5
	6			5	0
	3		1	0	0
	1		2	0	0
			3	0	0

2.

1	1	x		2	3
	5			4	6
	2			9	2
	1		1	8	4
			2	5	3

3.

1	7	x		3	0
	8			6	0
	4		1	2	0
	2		2	4	0
	1		4	8	0
			5	1	0

5.

2	1	x		5	0
1	0		1	0	0
	5		2	0	0
	2		4	0	0
	1		8	0	0
		1	0	5	0

4.

3	2	x		1	5
1	6			3	0
	8			6	0
	4		1	2	0
	2		2	4	0
	1		4	8	0
			4	8	0

6.

1	3	x		2	2
	6			4	4
	3			8	8
	1		1	7	6
			2	8	6

Chapter 8: Functions

Exercise 8.1: Finding outputs (1)

1. 14
2. 4
3. 14
4. 4
5. 7

6. 6
7. 26
8. 10
9. 4
10. 19

11. 4
12. 17
13. 19
14. 27
15. 2

16. 10
17. 9
18. 2
19. 18
20. 3

Exercise 8.2: Finding outputs (2)

1. 2
2. 24
3. 24
4. 4
5. 23

6. 15
7. 8
8. 4
9. 30
10. 21

11. 9
12. 10
13. 50
14. 100
15. 100

Exercise 8.3: Finding outputs using words

1. 13
2. 15
3. 42
4. 11
5. 5

6. 50
7. 2
8. 28
9. 4
10. 17

11. 10
12. 8
13. 12
14. 6
15. 200

Exercise 8.4: Finding inputs

1. (a) 8
   (b) 32
   (c) 8
   (d) 15
   (e) 7

   (f) 5
   (g) 9
   (h) 36
   (i) 15
   (j) 4

2.   (a) 3   (f) 20
       (b) 11   (g) 10
       (c) 21   (h) 18
       (d) 48   (i) 40
       (e) 25   (j) 22

Exercise 8.5: Summary exercise

1.   (a) 35   (d) 50
       (b) 15   (e) 27
       (c) 5   (f) 4

2.   (a) 108
       (b) 8

3.   (a) 16   (c) 34
       (b) 8   (d) 6

4.   (a) 63   (c) 49
       (b) 14   (d) 4

End of chapter activity: Missing digits (addition)

1.

	3	4
+	2	3
	5	7

4.

	1	8
+	**3**	8
	5	6

2.

	6	3
+	**2**	5
	8	8

5

		7	4
+		4	9
	1	2	3

3.

	4	7
+	2	5
	7	2

6.

		5	6
+		4	5
	1	0	1

7.

	1	3	6
+		6	2
	1	9	8

9.

	3	4	2
+	4	7	4
	8	1	6

8.

	2	1	7
+		4	7
	2	6	4

10.

		4	6	3
+		9	3	7
	1	4	0	0

Chapter 9: Inequalities

Exercise 9.1: Inequality signs

1. (a) seven is less than ten
    (b) eight is greater than two
    (c) nine plus one (ten) equals twelve minus two (ten)
    (d) five is greater than one
    (e) ten times two (twenty) is less than six times four (twenty-four)

2. (a) <
    (b) >
    (c) >
    (d) <
    (e) >

    (f) (10) > (5)
    (g) (5) < (11)
    (h) (16) > (4)
    (i) (5) = (5)
    (j) (5) < (10)

    (k) (14) < (15)
    (l) (6) > (2)
    (m) (21) = (21)

    (n) (20) < (50)
    (o) (4) < (6)

End of chapter activity: Missing digits (subtraction)

1.
	9	6
−	7	1
	2	5

4.
	6	0
−	1	7
	4	3

2.
	8	3
−	5	4
	2	9

5.
	7	4
−	2	5
	4	9

3.
	7	4
−	3	9
	3	5

6.
	6	3
−	3	8
	2	5

7.

	6	0	7
−	2	4	5
	3	6	2

8.

	4	3	1
−	2	1	4
	2	1	7

9.

	8	5	4
−	2	1	9
	6	3	5

10.

	8	4	1
−	1	9	6
	6	4	5

Chapter 10: Negative numbers

Exercise 10.1: Ordering positive and negative numbers

1.
(a) is less than
(b) is greater than
(c) is greater than
(d) is greater than
(e) is greater than

(f) is greater than
(g) is greater than
(h) is less than
(i) is less than
(j) is greater than

2.
(a) <
(b) >
(c) >
(d) <
(e) >

(f) <
(g) <
(h) <
(i) >
(j) >

3.
(a) True
(b) False
(c) False
(d) True

(e) True
(f) True
(g) False
(h) False

4.
(a)	⁻2	3	4	
(b)	⁻7	6	7	
(c)	⁻5	⁻4	4	
(d)	⁻2	0	2	
(e)	⁻6	⁻3	⁻1	
(f)	1	2	5	6
(g)	⁻6	⁻5	⁻2	⁻1
(h)	⁻8	⁻1	1	4
(i)	⁻1	0	1	2
(j)	⁻2	⁻1	0	2

5.
(a)	5	2	⁻3	
(b)	⁻1	⁻6	⁻8	
(c)	5	3	⁻4	
(d)	1	0	⁻1	
(e)	4	⁻2	⁻4	
(f)	7	4	2	1
(g)	⁻1	⁻2	⁻4	⁻7

(h) 8	5	⁻6	⁻7
(i) 9	4	0	⁻8
(j) 2	1	⁻1	⁻2

Exercise 10.2: Temperature changes

1.	10 °C	6.	⁻8 °C
2.	⁻3 °C	7.	10 °C
3.	4 °C	8.	6 °C
4.	1 °C	9.	11 °C
5.	⁻7 °C	10.	14 °C

Exercise 10.3: Summary exercise

1. (a) is greater than   (c) is less than
   (b) is less than   (d) is greater than

2. (a) <   (c) <
   (b) >   (d) >

3. (a) 1   0   ⁻2   ⁻6
   (b) 3   ⁻2   ⁻4   ⁻8

4. (a) ⁻6   ⁻4   ⁻1   3
   (b) ⁻4   ⁻2   1   3

5. 17 °C

6. 7 °C

End of chapter activity: Missing digits (multiplication)

1.
	2	3
×		4
	9	2

2.
	2	7
×		3
	8	1

3.
	3	7
×		2
	7	4

4.
		3	4
×			6
	2	0	4

5.

		5	6
x			7
	3	9	2

8.

		6	1
x			9
	5	4	**9**

6.

		2	**8**
x			5
	1	4	0

9.

		7	3
x			8
	5	8	4

7.

		3	9
x			**8**
	3	**1**	2

or

		4	9
x			**8**
	3	**9**	2

10.

		6	9
x			**7**
	4	8	3

Chapter 11: Sequences

Exercise 11.1: Sequences

1. (a)

    (b)

    (c)

    (d)

    (e)

2. (a) (i) add 2   (ii) 21   23
    (b) (i) subtract 3   (ii) 7   4
    (c) (i) add 7   (ii) 42   49
    (d) (i) subtract 12   (ii) 24   12
    (e) (i) divide by 10   (ii) 10   1
    (f) (i) add 2   (ii) 3   5
    (g) (i) subtract 2   (ii) 0   ⁻2
    (h) (i) subtract 5   (ii) ⁻4   ⁻9
    (i) (i) add 3   (ii) 0   3
    (j) (i) divide by 2   (ii) 2   1
    (k) (i) add 1, add 2, add 3 ...   (ii) 11   16
    (l) (i) add 1, add 3, add 5 ...   (ii) 17   26

(m) (i) subtract 1, subtract 2, subtract 3 ...   (ii) 10   5
(n) (i) square numbers   (ii) 25   36
(o) (i) Fibonacci sequence   (ii) 13   21

3. (a) 12   (n) 5
    (b) 6   (o) 60
    (c) 16   (p) 50
    (d) 10   (q) 150
    (e) 21   (r) 6   12
    (f) 11   (s) 9   3
    (g) 19   (t) 1   17
    (h) 8   (u) 26   21
    (i) 46   (v) 18   6
    (j) 4   (w) $^-$2   10
    (k) 29   (x) 7
    (l) 14   (y) 14
    (m) $^-$2

Exercise 11.2: Writing a sequence given a rule

1. 3   5   7   9   6. 6   3   0 $^-$3
2. 2   4   8   16   7. $^-$5 $^-$2 1   4
3. 24   20   16   12   8. 7   70   700   7000
4. 8   4   2   1   9. 49   38   27   16
5. 3   6   12   24   10. 25   50   75   100

11. 1   3   5   7   16. 2   8   20   44
12. 6   10   14   18   17. 5   9   17   33
13. 3   5   11   29   18. 5   8   14   26
14. 1   2   4   8   19. 1   6   21   66
15 2   6   14   30   20. 1   1   1   1

End of chapter activity: Pascal's triangle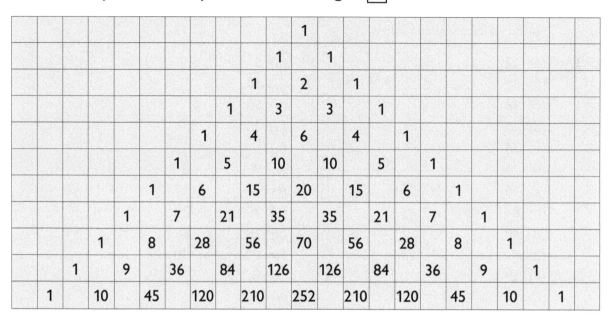

								1								
							1		1							
						1		2		1						
					1		3		3		1					
				1		4		6		4		1				
			1		5		10		10		5		1			
		1		6		15		20		15		6		1		
	1		7		21		35		35		21		7		1	
1		8		28		56		70		56		28		8		1
1		9		36		84		126		126		84		36		9		1
1	10	45	120	210	252	210	120	45	10	1

Some facts to notice about Pascal's triangle:

● Each line starts and ends with 1.
● Each number is the sum of the two numbers above it.
● The pattern is symmetrical about the centre.
● The total of each horizontal line is double the one above it.

Chapter 12: Money

Exercise 12.1: Conversion of money

1. (a) 400p
    (b) 700c
    (c) 1200c
    (d) 135p
    (e) 625c
    (f) 2415c

    (g) 40p
    (h) 95c
    (i) 8c
    (j) 10 000c
    (k) 5000c
    (l) 200 000p

2. (a) £9
    (b) €8
    (c) $17
    (d) £6.65
    (e) €1.48
    (f) $9.50

    (g) £0.95
    (h) €0.05
    (i) $0.10
    (j) £1.04
    (k) €1.40
    (l) $4.10

Exercise 12.2: Addition of money

1.   79p
2.   £1.33
3.   £1.16
4.   67p
5.   £1.27

6.   93p
7.   £1.90
8.   £2.23
9.   £2.42
10. £3.50

11. £4.69
12. £8.25
13. £9.85
14. $8.50
15. $15.15

16. £31.18
17. €6.75
18. €36.24
19. £6.75
20. £9.93

21. £33.51
22. €23.26
23. £3.25
24. £4.23
25. $22.30

26. £5.11
27. €2.00
28. £7.48
29. €35.26
30. $4.02

Exercise 12.3: Subtraction of money

1.	£1.61	6.	€2.84
2.	£5.23	7.	£1.61
3.	£1.58	8.	$1.84
4.	£4.48	9.	£2.63
5.	£6.48	10.	£3.58
11.	£2.57	16.	£8.73
12.	£6.55	17.	$22.70
13.	£4.63	18.	£21.60
14.	€5.72	19.	£45.64
15.	£22.75	20.	€62.71

Exercise 12.4: Multiplication of money

1.	51p	6.	£5.12
2.	£1.52	7.	£2.52
3.	£3.65	8.	£5.70
4.	£2.52	9.	£5.81
5.	£6.72	10.	£3.92
11.	£6.94	16.	£21.56
12.	£4.02	17.	£53.92
13.	$16.76	18.	€76.68
14.	£38.15	19.	£92.50
15.	€33.42	20.	$10.92
21.	£57.00	26.	$190.40
22.	$52.20	27	£534.20
23.	€82.50	28.	€430.90
24.	£43.50	29.	£205.96
25.	£156.90	30.	$311.90

Exercise 12.5: Division of money (1)

1.	17p		6.	38p
2.	17p		7.	24p
3.	17p		8.	15c
4.	24c		9.	27p
5.	13p		10.	27c

11.	63p		16.	69p
12.	72p		17.	17c
13.	87c		18.	34p
14.	73p		19.	72c
15.	45c		20.	75p

21.	£1.23		26.	£2.58
22.	£1.18		27.	$2.61
23.	$1.45		28.	£3.35
24.	£1.68		29.	£1.42
25.	€1.46		30.	€2.32

Exercise 12.6: Division of money (2)

1.	29p		6.	12p
2.	19p		7.	25c
3.	28c		8.	18p
4.	13p		9.	12p
5.	10c		10.	47c

11.	89p		16.	75c
12.	57p		17.	85p
13.	66p		18.	45p
14.	87c		19.	57c
15.	59p		20.	86p

21.	£1.88		26.	£2.79
22.	£1.29		27.	€2.43
23.	€1.52		28.	£2.63
24.	£1.74		29.	$2.47
25.	$1.59		30.	£3.39

31.	£5.45	**34.**	£3.50
32.	€4.68	**35.**	$2.12
33.	£2.18		

Exercise 12.7: One-step problems

1.	82p	**11.**	85p
2.	£1.14	**12.**	£5.34
3.	£3.55	**13.**	£35.20
4.	£4.35	**14.**	£1125
5.	$23.15	**15.**	€349.80
6.	27p	**16.**	45p
7.	73p	**17.**	$1.25
8.	£1.60	**18.**	£2.57
9.	€11.75	**19.**	£9.40
10.	£49.99	**20.**	£6.50

Exercise 12.8: Two-step problems

1. The offer. 24p cheaper.
2. £405
3. £9.75
4. £1.25
5. £5.00
6. £1.65
7. €2.68
8. No. 30c short. Buy 1 waffle fewer.
9. (a) £8.55
    (b) £11.45
10. £3.70

End of chapter activity: Money round the world

Check pupils' answers.

Chapter 13: Fractions

Exercise 13.1: Writing improper fractions as whole numbers or mixed numbers

1. (a) 1
    (b) 1
    (c) 5
    (d) 3
    (e) 2

    (f) 3
    (g) 6
    (h) 3
    (i) 4
    (j) 3

2. (a) $1\frac{1}{6}$

    (b) $1\frac{3}{7}$

    (c) $1\frac{3}{8}$

    (d) $1\frac{3}{10}$

    (e) $1\frac{4}{5}$

    (f) $2\frac{1}{3}$

    (g) $2\frac{3}{5}$

    (h) $2\frac{3}{4}$

    (i) $2\frac{3}{7}$

    (j) $2\frac{2}{9}$

    (k) $3\frac{1}{6}$

    (l) $3\frac{3}{10}$

    (m) $2\frac{5}{8}$

    (n) $4\frac{4}{5}$

    (o) $6\frac{1}{2}$

    (p) $7\frac{2}{3}$

    (q) $6\frac{3}{4}$

    (r) $6\frac{5}{6}$

    (s) $4\frac{3}{8}$

    (t) $4\frac{9}{10}$

3. (a) $1\frac{1}{2}$ (f) $1\frac{1}{4}$

(b) $1\frac{1}{3}$ (g) $1\frac{1}{5}$

(c) $2\frac{1}{2}$ (h) $1\frac{1}{5}$

(d) $2\frac{2}{3}$ (i) $1\frac{1}{2}$

(e) $2\frac{3}{5}$ (j) $1\frac{3}{4}$

(k) $1\frac{2}{7}$ (n) $1\frac{2}{5}$

(l) $1\frac{3}{8}$ (o) $1\frac{1}{4}$

(m) $1\frac{1}{2}$

Exercise 13.2: Fractions and division

1. $1\frac{5}{7}$ **6.** $3\frac{2}{9}$

2. $2\frac{4}{5}$ **7.** $4\frac{3}{4}$

3. $2\frac{1}{8}$ **8.** $4\frac{1}{6}$

4. $5\frac{5}{6}$ **9.** $3\frac{2}{7}$

5. $3\frac{4}{5}$ **10.** $3\frac{7}{10}$

Exercise 13.3: Writing mixed numbers as improper fractions

1. $\frac{3}{2}$ **6.** $\frac{13}{5}$

2. $\frac{7}{4}$ **7.** $\frac{31}{12}$

3. $\frac{17}{10}$ **8.** $\frac{41}{15}$

4. $\frac{11}{6}$ **9.** $\frac{19}{5}$

5. $\frac{8}{3}$ **10.** $\frac{34}{9}$

11. $\frac{39}{10}$

16. $\frac{17}{3}$

12. $\frac{14}{3}$

17. $\frac{41}{7}$

13. $\frac{32}{7}$

18. $\frac{53}{9}$

14. $\frac{43}{10}$

19. $\frac{49}{8}$

15. $\frac{52}{11}$

20. $\frac{15}{2}$

21. $\frac{25}{6}$

26. $\frac{41}{12}$

22. $\frac{25}{3}$

27. $\frac{44}{9}$

23. $\frac{39}{20}$

28. $\frac{27}{4}$

24. $\frac{43}{15}$

29. $\frac{22}{3}$

25. $\frac{57}{25}$

30. $\frac{53}{5}$

Exercise 13.4: Ordering fractions (1)

1. (a) $\frac{5}{8}$ $\frac{1}{2}$ (f) $\frac{11}{18}$ $\frac{5}{9}$

    (b) $\frac{7}{12}$ $\frac{1}{2}$ (g) $\frac{9}{10}$ $\frac{17}{20}$

    (c) $\frac{5}{6}$ $\frac{2}{3}$ (h) $\frac{3}{4}$ $\frac{13}{20}$

    (d) $\frac{3}{4}$ $\frac{7}{12}$ (i) $\frac{7}{15}$ $\frac{1}{3}$

    (e) $\frac{3}{8}$ $\frac{1}{4}$ (j) $\frac{13}{16}$ $\frac{3}{4}$

2. (a) $\frac{5}{6}$ $\frac{11}{12}$ (f) $\frac{5}{8}$ $\frac{11}{16}$

    (b) $\frac{1}{3}$ $\frac{4}{9}$ (g) $\frac{3}{15}$ $\frac{2}{3}$

    (c) $\frac{4}{5}$ $\frac{9}{10}$ (h) $\frac{1}{4}$ $\frac{7}{20}$

    (d) $\frac{13}{18}$ $\frac{5}{6}$ (i) $\frac{7}{24}$ $\frac{1}{3}$

    (e) $\frac{11}{14}$ $\frac{6}{7}$ (j) $\frac{5}{7}$ $\frac{17}{21}$

Exercise 13.5: Lowest common multiple

1.	6	**5.**	30
2.	12	**6.**	12
3.	12	**7.**	40
4.	18	**8.**	24
9.	12	**13.**	12
10.	6	**14.**	24
11.	24	**15.**	36
12.	30		

Exercise 13.6: Ordering fractions (2)

1. (a) $\frac{2}{3}$ (f) $\frac{3}{4}$

(b) $\frac{2}{5}$ (g) $\frac{2}{3}$

(c) $\frac{3}{4}$ (h) $\frac{7}{12}$

(d) $\frac{9}{10}$ (i) $\frac{7}{10}$

(e) $\frac{1}{2}$ (j) $\frac{9}{10}$

2. (a) $\frac{3}{4}$ $\frac{5}{8}$ $\frac{1}{2}$

(b) $\frac{4}{5}$ $\frac{3}{4}$ $\frac{7}{10}$

(c) $\frac{11}{12}$ $\frac{7}{8}$ $\frac{3}{4}$

(d) $\frac{7}{8}$ $\frac{4}{5}$ $\frac{3}{4}$

(e) $\frac{1}{3}$ $\frac{2}{9}$ $\frac{1}{6}$

3. (a) $\frac{4}{9}$ (f) $\frac{5}{8}$

(b) $\frac{1}{3}$ (g) $\frac{1}{6}$

(c) $\frac{2}{3}$ (h) $\frac{2}{3}$

(d) $\frac{3}{4}$ (i) $\frac{4}{5}$

(e) $\frac{2}{3}$ (j) $\frac{3}{4}$

4. (a) $\frac{2}{3}$ $\frac{3}{4}$ $\frac{5}{6}$

(b) $\frac{8}{15}$ $\frac{2}{3}$ $\frac{4}{5}$

(c) $\frac{4}{9}$ $\frac{1}{2}$ $\frac{2}{3}$

(d) $\frac{7}{12}$ $\frac{2}{3}$ $\frac{3}{4}$

(e) $\frac{1}{2}$ $\frac{3}{5}$ $\frac{2}{3}$

Exercise 13.7: Summary exercise

1. (a) $4\frac{1}{2}$ (d) $2\frac{3}{8}$

(b) $2\frac{4}{5}$*   (e) $3\frac{1}{2}$

(c) $6\frac{3}{4}$

> *The answer given here is for the correct fraction $\frac{14}{5}$
>
> The fraction given in the first printing of the pupil's book is $\frac{14}{15}$ and should read $\frac{14}{5}$

2. (a) $5\frac{1}{2}$ (d) $3\frac{1}{7}$

(b) $4\frac{3}{5}$ (e) $7\frac{1}{2}$

(c) $4\frac{2}{7}$

3. (a) $\frac{5}{3}$ (d) $\frac{13}{5}$

(b) $\frac{7}{2}$ (e) $\frac{37}{8}$

(c) $\frac{23}{4}$

4. (a) 12

(b) 24

(c) 18

(d) 12

(e) 12

(f) 30

(g) 24

(h) 15

5. (a) $\frac{11}{16}$ $\frac{5}{8}$

(b) $\frac{5}{7}$ $\frac{2}{3}$

(c) $\frac{4}{5}$ $\frac{3}{4}$

(d) $\frac{3}{5}$ $\frac{8}{15}$ $\frac{1}{2}$

(e) $\frac{3}{4}$ $\frac{2}{3}$ $\frac{7}{12}$

6. (a) $\frac{5}{9}$ $\frac{2}{3}$

(b) $\frac{3}{4}$ $\frac{4}{5}$

(c) $\frac{5}{6}$ $\frac{7}{8}$

(d) $\frac{2}{3}$ $\frac{5}{6}$ $\frac{8}{9}$

(e) $\frac{3}{10}$ $\frac{1}{3}$ $\frac{2}{5}$

End of chapter activity: Four and twenty

Possible answer:

0. $4 - 4$

1. $4 \div 4$

2. $\frac{4}{4} + \frac{4}{4}$

3. $4 - \frac{4}{4}$

4. 4

5. $4 + \frac{4}{4}$

6. $4 + \frac{4}{4} + \frac{4}{4}$

7. $4 + 4 - \frac{4}{4}$

8. $4 + 4$

9. $4 + 4 + \frac{4}{4}$

10. $\frac{44}{4} - \frac{4}{4}$

11. $\frac{44}{4}$

12. $4 + 4 + 4$

13. $4 + 4 + 4 + \frac{4}{4}$

14. $4 \times 4 - \frac{4}{4} - \frac{4}{4}$

15. $\frac{44}{4} + 4$

16. 4×4

17. $4 \times 4 + \frac{4}{4}$

18. $4 \times 4 + \frac{4}{4} + \frac{4}{4}$

19. $4 \times 4 + 4 - \frac{4}{4}$

20. $4 \times (4 + \frac{4}{4})$

Answer depends on what the children know ($\sqrt{4} = 2$ is useful if known!).

Chapter 14: Introduction to decimals

Exercise 14.1: Place value and decimals

1. $\frac{3}{10}$

2. $\frac{7}{100}$

3. $\frac{7}{1000}$

4. $\frac{3}{100}$

5. $\frac{1}{1000}$

6. $\frac{7}{10}$

7. $\frac{9}{1000}$

8. $\frac{9}{10}$

9. $\frac{9}{100}$

10. $\frac{7}{10}$

11. $\frac{9}{100}$

12. $\frac{7}{1000}$

13. $\frac{3}{10}$

14. 6

15. $\frac{3}{100}$

16. $\frac{7}{1000}$

17. 20

18. $\frac{1}{10}$

19. 200

20. $\frac{3}{100}$

21. $\frac{3}{10}$

22. 80

23. 4000

24. $\frac{7}{1000}$

25. 2

Exercise 14.2: Ordering decimals (1)

1.　(a) 0.8

　　(b) 0.62

　　(c) 0.5

　　(d) 0.7

　　(e) 0.75

2.　(a) 0.2

　　(b) 0.49

　　(c) 0.21

　　(d) 0.05

　　(e) 0.01

Exercise 14.3: Ordering decimals (2)

1.　(a)　0.5　　　0.6　　　0.7

　　(b)　0.71　　0.73　　0.74

　　(c)　0.8　　　0.82　　0.87

　　(d)　0.502　0.55　　0.6

　　(e)　0.07　　0.62　　0.7

　　(f)　0.17　　0.32　　0.406　　0.5

　　(g)　0.09　　0.123　0.14　　0.25

　　(h)　0.012　0.102　0.12　　0.21

　　(i)　0.054　0.45　　0.504　　0.54

　　(j)　0.17　　0.71　　1.07　　7.1

2. (a) 0.19   0.16   0.15

     (b) 0.68   0.66   0.64

     (c) 0.31   0.3   0.29

     (d) 0.97   0.2   0.106

     (e) 0.201   0.102   0.021

     (f) 0.8   0.41   0.306   0.17

     (g) 0.242   0.1   0.09   0.07

     (h) 0.63   0.603   0.36   0.063

     (i) 0.491   0.419   0.194   0.149

     (j) 213   21.3   2.13   0.213

Exercise 14.4: Writing decimals as fractions (1)

1. $\frac{3}{10}$ **6.** $\frac{7}{10}$

2. $\frac{61}{100}$ **7.** $4\frac{23}{100}$

3. $\frac{127}{1000}$ **8.** $62\frac{83}{100}$

4. $\frac{77}{100}$ **9.** $1\frac{369}{1000}$

5. $\frac{707}{1000}$ **10.** $8\frac{1}{10}$

Exercise 14.5: Writing decimals as fractions (2)

1. $\frac{3}{5}$ **6.** $\frac{3}{20}$

2. $\frac{4}{5}$ **7.** $\frac{1}{4}$

3. $\frac{1}{2}$ **8.** $\frac{9}{50}$

4. $\frac{7}{50}$ **9.** $\frac{2}{5}$

5. $\frac{3}{25}$ **10.** $\frac{23}{50}$

11. $\frac{4}{25}$

12. $\frac{7}{20}$

13. $\frac{31}{50}$

14. $\frac{11}{25}$

15. $\frac{9}{20}$

16. $\frac{8}{25}$

17. $\frac{37}{50}$

18. $\frac{6}{25}$

19. $\frac{19}{20}$

20. $\frac{3}{4}$

21. $\frac{1}{50}$

22. $\frac{1}{25}$

23. $\frac{1}{20}$

24. $3\frac{1}{5}$

25. $1\frac{13}{50}$

Exercise 14.6: Summary exercise

1. (a) $\frac{9}{100}$

   (b) 20

   (c) $\frac{7}{1000}$

   (d) $\frac{3}{10}$

   (e) 6

2. (a) 0.9   0.86   0.75   0.72

   (b) 0.33   0.32   0.313   0.033

   (c) 1.7   0.79   0.759   0.7

3. (a) 0.45   0.53   0.69   0.96

     (b) 0.004   0.4   0.426   0.46

     (c) 3.15   3.51   5.23   5.32

4. (a) $\frac{3}{5}$ (e) $\frac{1}{4}$

     (b) $\frac{3}{20}$ (f) $\frac{11}{25}$

     (c) $\frac{31}{50}$ (g) $\frac{2}{25}$

     (d) $\frac{1}{2}$ (h) $\frac{7}{10}$

End of chapter activity: Dominoes

Practical. Cut the dominoes out from the worksheet or challenge pupils to make their own.

Chapter 15: Decimal addition and subtraction

Exercise 15.1: Adding decimals

1. 8.8
2. 8.3
3. 17.9
4. 15.2
5. 58.4

6. 88.5
7. 148.8
8. 48.3
9. 104.3
10. 128.2

11. 11.7
12. 16.9
13. 13.5
14. 26.3
15. 2.2

16. 10.55
17. 13.32
18. 96.6
19. 85.7
20. 82.7

21. 30.66
22. 50.28
23. 11.65
24. 5.56
25. 3.335

26. 32.6
27. 72.3
28. 12.75
29. 35.6
30. 51.83

31. 45.83
32. 44.75
33. 39.16
34. 19.314
35. 48.396

36. 65
37. 15.19
38. 15.8
39. 181.2
40. 558.33

Exercise 15.2: Subtracting decimals

1. 3.4
2. 4.4
3. 0.6
4. 1.18
5. 4.85

6. 6.67
7. 31.7
8. 25.2
9. 16.7
10. 9.2

11. 6.65
12. 28.2
13. 4.13
14. 12.7
15. 2.73

16. 1.96
17. 24.9
18. 3.32
19. 1.07
20. 4.146

21. 21.18
22. 91.63
23. 77.44
24. 5.54
25. 1.842

26. 71.8
27. 66.6
28. 32.178
29. 17.63
30. 33.24

31. 5.53
32. 0.364
33. 366.14
34. 232.2
35. 1.629

Exercise 15.3: Summary exercise

1. (a) 7.33 (d) 26.5
   (b) 27.27 (e) 50.93
   (c) 53.1

2. (a) 16.7 (d) 6.35
   (b) 33.77 (e) 76.5
   (c) 33.8

3. (a) 4.8 (f) 74.6
   (b) 5.4 (g) 9.42
   (c) 9.1 (h) 16.34
   (d) 2.8 (i) 18.97
   (e) 8.4 (j) 23.46

End of chapter activity: Missing digits (division)

1.

	3	4	
2	6	8	

6.

		4	3
6	2	5	8

2.

	3	2	
3	9	6	

7.

		4	0
9	3	6	0

3.

		3	7
5	1	8	5

8.

		8	1
7	5	6	7

4.

		5	1
8	4	0	8

9.

		4	3
3	1	2	9

5.

		7	2
4	2	8	8

10.

		1	9	7
5	9	8	5	

Chapter 16: Scales, estimation and rounding

Exercise 16.1: Reading scales

1. A = 200   B = 500   C = 650

2. A = 400   B = 700   C = 850

3. A = 0.1   B = 0.6   C = 0.95

4. A = 0.8   B = 0.3   C = 0.15

5. A = 1200   B = 1450   C = 1725

6. A = 4200   B = 4500   C = 4850

7. A = 1.4   B = 1.7   C = 1.55

8. A = 4.4   B = 4.1   C = 4.75

Exercise 16.2: Marking numbers on a scale

1.

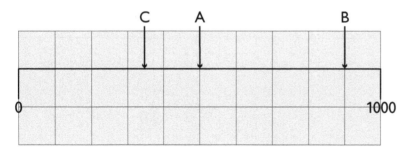

2.

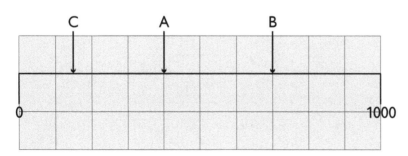

3.

4.

5.

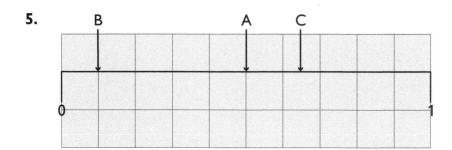

6.

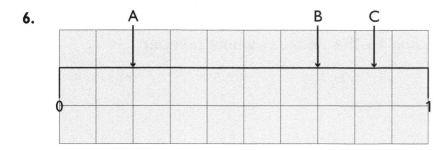

7.

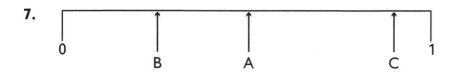

8.

Exercise 16.3: Rounding to the nearest 1000

1.   (a) 3000   (b) 4000   (c) 7000   (d) 8000   (e) 2000

2.   4000 miles

3.   8000 votes

4.   9000 metres

5.   4000 days

6.   £6000

7.   3000 turkeys

8.   2000

9.   9000 hours

10.   10 000 miles

Exercise 16.4: Rounding to the nearest whole number

1.   (a) 9   (b) 7   (c) 3   (d) 6   (e) 3

2.   3 kilograms

3.   7 °C

4.   11 seconds

5.   2 metres

6.   £27

7.   49 centimetres

8.   37 °C, 98 °F

9.   8 cups

10.   124 centimetres

Exercise 16.5: Summary exercise

1. (a) A = 0.5   B = 0.2   C = 0.85

    (b) A = 6   B = 1   C = 7.5

    (c) A = 40   B = 70   C = 15

    (d) A = 300   B = 450   C = 625

    (e) A = 3800   B = 3300   C = 3550

    (f) A = 6.4   B = 6.7   C = 6.25

2. (a)

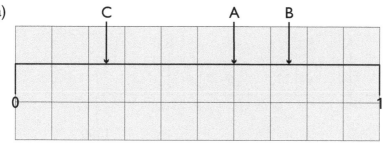

    (b)

    (c)

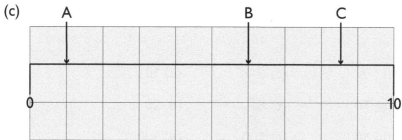

    (d)

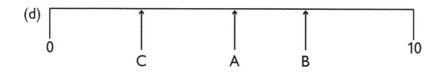

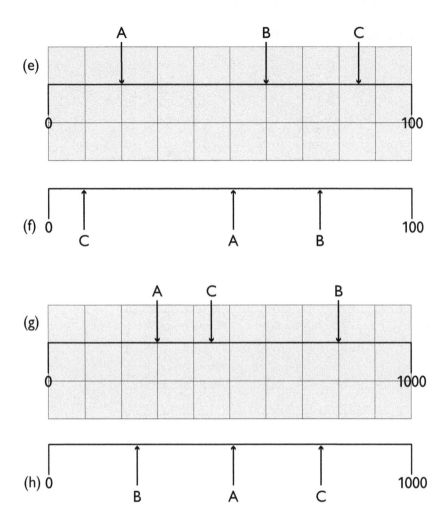

3. (a) 5   (b) 3   (c) 8   (d) 10

4. (a) 40   (b) 70   (c) 80   (d) 20

5. (a) 100   (b) 500   (c) 900   (d) 300

6. (a) 8000   (b) 6000   (c) 9000   (d) 4000

End of chapter activity: Palindromes

Examples:

1 stage: 18   24   35   42   53   63   72   81   90

2 stage: 19   37   49   57   64   75   82   93

3 stage: 59   68   86   95

4 stage: 69   78   87   96

79 and 97 need 6 stages

89 and 98 need 24 stages

Don't forget single digits and numbers that repeat a digit (11, 22, etc) need 0 stages since they are palindromes to start with.

Chapter 17: Multiplication and division by 10, 100 and 1000

Exercise 17.1: Multiplying whole numbers by 10, 100 and 1000

1. 70
2. 460
3. 8040
4. 10 700
5. 600

6. 4900
7. 30 000
8. 123 400
9. 9000
10. 37 000

11. 716 000
12. 1 000 000
13. 4700
14. 380
15. 5000

16. 72 000
17. 700
18. 2000
19. 200 000
20. 1250

Exercise 17.2: Multiplying decimals by 10, 100 and 1000

1. (a) 43
   (b) 286.4

   (c) 1.9
   (d) 8

2. (a) 463.2
   (b) 386
   (c) 87.2

   (d) 4.23
   (e) 0.16
   (f) 170

3. (a) 1295
   (b) 326.7
   (c) 12 329
   (d) 87

   (e) 400
   (f) 23 420
   (g) 240
   (h) 365

4. (a) 17.5

(b) 338

(c) 2550

(d) 8

(e) 0.7

(f) 7293

(g) 142.5

(h) 345

(i) 960

(j) 1.4

(k) 10

(l) 1

(m) 2720

(n) 0.6

(o) 7050

(p) 840

(q) 387.5

(r) 2600

(s) 29.5

(t) 4.05

Exercise 17.3: Dividing by 10, 100 and 1000 (whole number answers)

1. 7

2. 12

3. 800

4. 4

5. 80

6. 430

7. 2

8. 38

9. 120

10. 1000

Exercise 17.4: Dividing by 10, 100 and 1000 (decimal answers)

1. (a) 1.86

(b) 0.63

(c) 1.9

(d) 83.5

(e) 230

(f) 0.3

2. (a) 1.482

(b) 0.387

(c) 17

(d) 3.65

(e) 151.3

(f) 0.62

(g) 0.064

(h) 0.09

3.   (a) 4.865   (e) 0.425

       (b) 27.9   (f) 0.005

       (c) 0.7875   (g) 0.0184

       (d) 2.5   (h) 0.0072

4.   (a) 3.24   (g) 28.74

       (b) 1.234   (h) 0.78

       (c) 3.2179   (i) 0.83

       (d) 29.8   (j) 0.409

       (e) 3.5   (k) 0.6

       (f) 2.756   (l) 0.5

       (m) 0.284   (s) 0.009

       (n) 0.06   (t) 0.0002

       (o) 0.0015   (u) 0.027

       (p) 0.008   (v) 0.0004

       (q) 0.0355   (w) 0.007

       (r) 0.046   (x) 0.01

Exercise 17.5: Summary exercise

1.	650	**6.**	1000
2.	7	**7.**	286
3.	453.2	**8.**	70
4.	0.65	**9.**	491.5
5.	94.5	**10.**	30 700
11.	70 000	**16.**	3.3
12.	875	**17.**	0.426
13.	4340	**18.**	87.6
14.	10	**19.**	0.7
15.	28 900	**20.**	0.006

21.	57.8	**26.**	1.247
22.	1.737	**27.**	0.0238
23.	0.27	**28.**	0.009
24.	0.01	**29.**	0.246 95
25.	2.5	**30.**	0.000 23

End of chapter activity: Mrs Chick

36 eggs and 5 baskets.

If you put 7 eggs in each of 5 baskets there is 1 egg left over.

If you put 9 eggs in a basket you fill 4 baskets exactly.

Chapter 18: Metric measurement

Exercise 18.1: Converting length (1)

1. (a) 80 mm
   (b) 150 mm
   (c) 68 mm
   (d) 32.5 mm
   (e) 5 mm

2. (a) 200 cm
   (b) 1500 cm
   (c) 475 cm
   (d) 130 cm
   (e) 50 cm

3. (a) 3000 mm
   (b) 10 000 mm
   (c) 1250 mm
   (d) 2700 mm
   (e) 500 mm

4. (a) 8000 m
   (b) 25 000 m
   (c) 4750 m
   (d) 7900 m
   (e) 500 m

5. (a) 70 mm
   (b) 3000 m
   (c) 600 cm
   (d) 6000 mm
   (e) 88 mm
   (f) 430 cm
   (g) 85 cm
   (h) 11 600 m
   (i) 750 mm
   (j) 120 mm

Exercise 18.2: Converting length (2)

1. (a) 6 cm
   (b) 3.8 cm
   (c) 30 cm
   (d) 0.8 cm

2. (a) 7 m
   (b) 12.5 m
   (c) 0.3 m
   (d) 0.07 m

3. (a) 9 m
   (b) 5.5 m
   (c) 0.75 m
   (d) 0.085 m

4. (a) 3 km
   (b) 25 km
   (c) 0.4 km
   (d) 0.11 km

5. (a) 0.25 m
    (b) 12 km
    (c) 0.745 m
    (d) 7.5 cm
    (e) 1.5 km

    (f) 1.27 m
    (g) 0.08 km
    (h) 2.8 m
    (i) 0.1 cm
    (j) 0.01 m

Exercise 18.3: Converting mass (1)

1. (a) 2000 mg
    (b) 12 000 mg

    (c) 3500 mg
    (d) 600 mg

2. (a) 6000 g
    (b) 14 200 g

    (c) 800 g
    (d) 5350 g

3. (a) 3000 kg
    (b) 6700 kg

    (c) 250 kg
    (d) 12 000 kg

4. (a) 6000 mg
    (b) 8000 g
    (c) 15 000 kg
    (d) 2750 g
    (e) 7125 kg

    (f) 600 g
    (g) 1700 kg
    (h) 10 500 mg
    (i) 385 g
    (j) 80 kg

Exercise 18.4: Converting mass (2)

1. (a) 6 g
    (b) 3.7 g

    (c) 12 g
    (d) 0.95 g

2. (a) 2 kg
    (b) 0.575 kg

    (c) 1.4 kg
    (d) 0.05 kg

3. (a) 3 t
    (b) 1.02 t

    (c) 0.7 t
    (d) 120 t

4. (a) 9 t
    (b) 1.2 kg
    (c) 15 g
    (d) 5.05 t
    (e) 0.454 kg

    (f) 1.85 g
    (g) 0.4 t
    (h) 0.05 t
    (i) 0.1 kg
    (j) 0.01 g

Exercise 18.5: Converting capacity

1. (a) 5000 *ml*   (c) 330 *ml*
    (b) 7500 *ml*   (d) 12 000 *ml*

2. (a) 9 *l*   (c) 0.4 *l*
    (b) 1.3 *l*   (d) 50.5 *l*

Exercise 18.6: Problem solving

Length

1. (a) 1600 m   (b) 1.6 km

2. 37.2 km

3. 20 m

4. 15 staples

5. 3.3 m

Mass

6. (a) 1575 g   (b) 1.575 kg

7. 840 g

8. 150 kg

9. 125 g

10. (a) 3500 kg   (b) 3.5 t

Capacity

11. 17.5 *l*

12. 1.7 *l*

13. 30 *l*

14. 19 times

15. 300 *ml* more

Exercise 18.7: Summary exercise

1. (a) 48 mm
    (b) 500 cm
    (c) 1500 mm
    (d) 10 800 m
    (e) 4000 mg

    (f) 3750 g
    (g) 600 kg
    (h) 6875 *ml*
    (i) 0.04 *l*
    (j) 43 t

    (k) 0.9 kg
    (l) 13.5 g
    (m) 0.8 km
    (n) 1.2 m
    (o) 0.5 m

    (p) 8.5 cm
    (q) 1.3 m
    (r) 13 cm
    (s) 0.01 kg
    (t) 10 000 g

2. (a) 1400 g

    (b) 1.4 kg

3. 28 cm

4. (a) 4200 *ml*

    (b) 4.2 *l*

5. (a) 22.5 mm

    (b) 2.25 cm

6. (a) 25 coins

    (b) £12.50

7. (a) 6 *l*

    (b) 24 glasses

8. 125 g

9. (a) 3.5 kg

    (b) £35

10. (a) Yes.

    (b) There is 5 mm to spare

11. Between 4 and 5 litres (4.56 *l*)

End of chapter activity: Traffic control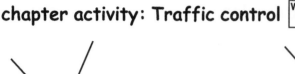

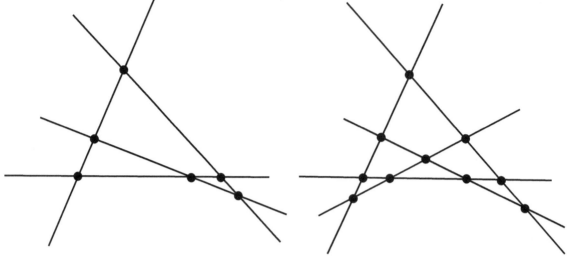

Streets	Policemen
1	0
2	1
3	3
4	6
5	10
6	15
7	21

The numbers in the 'policemen' column are the triangular numbers. Add 1 to the first number (0), then add 2, then 3, then 4, and so on.

Chapter 19: Lines

Exercise 19.1: Measuring lines

1.	9.5 cm	6.	11.9 cm
2.	5.3 cm	7.	10.0 cm
3.	8.7 cm	8.	6.1 cm
4.	4.8 cm	9.	9.2 cm
5.	7.4 cm	10.	3.6 cm

Exercise 19.2: Drawing lines

Check pupils' answers.

End of chapter activity: More lines

Check pupils' answers. Pupils could use the internet and this activity could be used as a basis for group work and class discussion.

Chapter 20: Position – co-ordinates

Exercise 20.1: Reading co-ordinates (1)

A = (1, 2)   F = (8, 1)

B = (2, 4)   G = (5, 3)

C = (4, 7)   H = (3, 5)

D = (6, 8)   I = (0, 1)

E = (7, 6)   J = (1, 0)

Exercise 20.2: Reading co-ordinates (2)

A = (2, 8)   F = (3, 1)

B = (4, 5)   G = (1, 2)

C = (5, 4)   H = (0, 7)

D = (7, 3)   I = (5, 7)

E = (6, 0)   J = (8, 6)

Exercise 20.3: Plotting points

1.

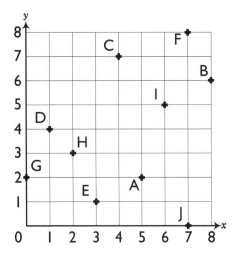

2.

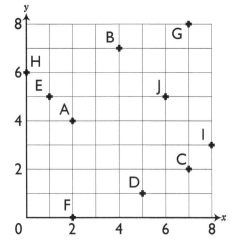

Exercise 20.4: Drawing shapes

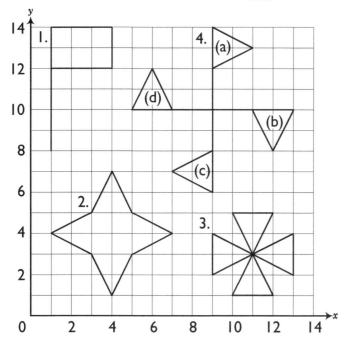

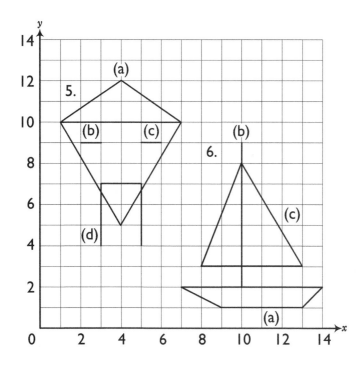

Exercise 20.5: Drawing shapes with letters

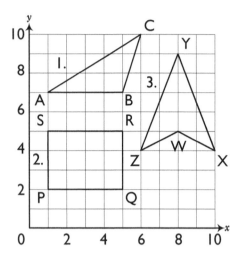

4. ABC = scalene triangle

PQRS = rectangle

WXYZ = arrowhead

End of chapter activity: Making squares

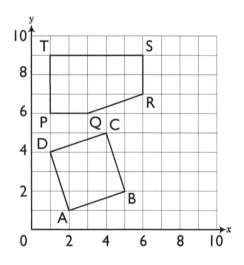

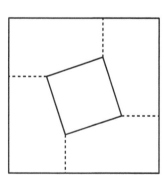

Chapter 21: Angles and direction

Exercise 21.1: Types of angle

1. acute
2. acute
3. right
4. obtuse
5. obtuse
6. acute
7. right
8. acute
9. obtuse
10. acute
11. obtuse
12. acute

Exercise 21.2: Measuring angles (1)

1. 40°
2. 60°
3. 30°
4. 70°
5. 110°
6. 140°
7. 130°
8. 120°
9. 50°
10. 100°
11. 100°
12. 80°

Exercise 21.3: Measuring angles (2)

1. 35°
2. 55°
3. 105°
4. 115°
5. 45°
6. 25°
7. 75°
8. 95°
9. 125°
10. 65°
11. 105°
12. 135°

Exercise 21.4: Drawing angles

Check pupils' answers.

Exercise 21.5: Angles and the hands of a clock

1. (a) 60°
    (b) 90°
    (c) 210°

    (d) 300°
    (e) 15°

2. (a) 30°
    (b) 90°
    (c) 150°

    (d) 180°
    (e) 45°

Exercise 21.6: Direction – the compass

1. (a) 45°
    (b) 135°
    (c) 225°
    (d) 315°
    (e) 135°
    (f) 225°
    (g) 45°
    (h) 135°

    (i) 90°
    (j) 90°
    (k) 90°
    (l) 90°
    (m) 180°
    (n) 180°
    (o) 270°

2. (a) (8, 12)
    (b) (7, 8)
    (c) (13, 8)
    (d) (8, 2)
    (e) (5, 5)
    (f) (13, 13)
    (g) (14, 2)
    (h) (6, 10)
    (i) (9, 12)
    (j) (5, 1)

    (k) (7, 15)
    (l) (13, 10)
    (m) (10, 14)
    (n) (9, 1)
    (o) (1, 11)
    (p) (15, 11)
    (q) (9, 5)
    (r) (6, 8)
    (s) (2, 10)
    (t) (7, 8)

3. (a) 4 west
    (b) 4 south
    (c) 6 north
    (d) 6 east
    (e) 6 south-east

    (f) 4 north-west
    (g) 7 north-east
    (h) 8 south-west
    (i) 4 north, 1 west or vice versa
    (j) 3 south, 1 east or vice versa

Exercise 21.7: Summary exercise

1. (a) 80°
    (b) 100°
    (c) 25°
    (d) 105°

2. Check pupils' answers.

3. (a) 30°
    (b) 120°

4. (a) 45°
    (b) 135°

5. (a) (3, 6)
    (b) (0, 6)
    (c) (7, 2)
    (d) 5 squares south
    (e) 6 squares north-east

End of chapter activity: Clock shapes

Shape 1
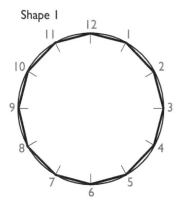

Shape 2
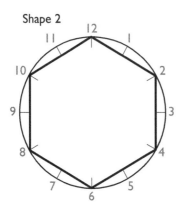

Shape 3
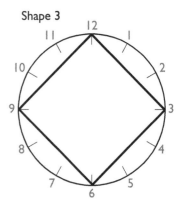

Shape 4
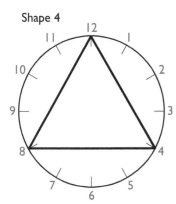

Shape 5
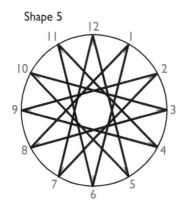

Shape 6
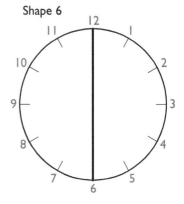

Shape 7
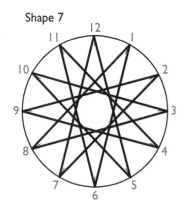

Shapes 5 and 7 are the same.

Shape 8 will be the same as shape 4.

Shape 9 will be the same as shape 3.

And so on.

Chapter 22: 2D shapes

Exercise 22.1: 2D shapes

1. (a) semicircle   (b) parallelogram   (c) arrowhead   (d) pentagon

2. (a)    (c)

   (b) 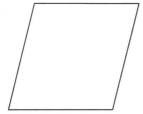   (d)

3. (a) square
   (b) isosceles triangle
   (c) trapezium
   (d) scalene triangle

4. radius

5. equilateral

6. all sides and all angles are equal

7. 10

8. octagon

9. lines that are equidistant (always the same distant apart)

10. (a) 2
    (b) square, rectangle
    (c) square, kite, rhombus
    (d) square, rectangle, rhombus, parallelogram

Exercise 22.2: Shapes on a grid

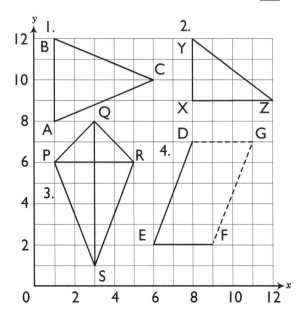

1. (a) see grid
   (b) isosceles

2. (a) see grid
   (b) right-angled scalene
   (c) acute
   (d) 5 cm

3. (a) see grid
   (b) kite
   (c) see grid
   (d) 90°

4. (a), (b), (c) see grid
   (d) (11, 7)

End of chapter activity: Diagonals

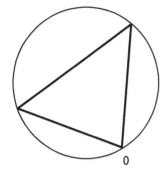

0

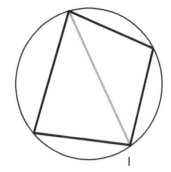

1

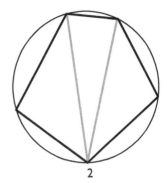

2

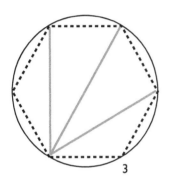

3

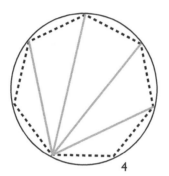

4

Shape	Sides	Number of vertices	Number of diagonals from one vertex
Triangle	3	3	0
Quadrilateral	4	4	1
Pentagon	5	5	2
Hexagon	6	6	3
Heptagon	7	7	4

The number of diagonals is 3 less than the number of sides/vertices.

An octagon has 5 diagonals.

A decagon has 7 diagonals.

A 50-sided figure has 47 diagonals.

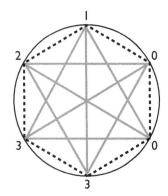 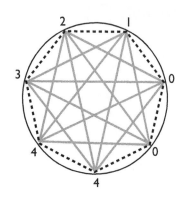

Shape	Sides	Number of diagonals from one vertex	Total number of diagonals
Triangle	3	0	0
Quadrilateral	4	1	2
Pentagon	5	2	5
Hexagon	6	3	9
Heptagon	7	4	14
Octagon	8	5	20
Decagon	10	7	35

Chapter 23: Symmetry and reflection

Exercise 23.1: Symmetry

1. (a) (i) EP   (ii) CQ

   (b) PA = PF or QB = QE

   (c) angle PEQ = x, angle BQC = y

   (d) They are congruent

2. (a)

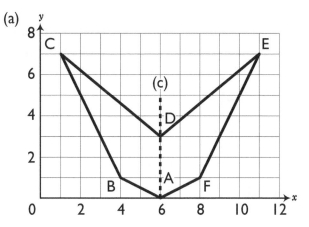

   (b) hexagon

   (c) see grid

   (d) (i) AB   (ii) FE

   (e) angle B

   (f) triangle AFD

3. (a)

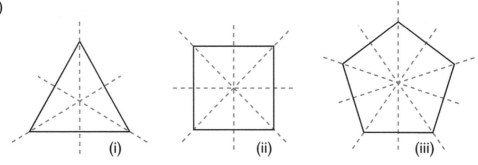

(i) (ii) (iii)

(b)

	Name of shape	Number of sides	Number of lines of symmetry
(i)	Equilateral triangle	3	3
(ii)	Square	4	4
(iii)	Regular pentagon	5	5

(c) All the sides of each shape are equal.

(d) They are the same.

(e) 10 lines of symmetry, because 10 sides.

Exercise 23.2: Reflection

1. (a)

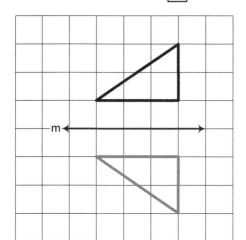

(d)

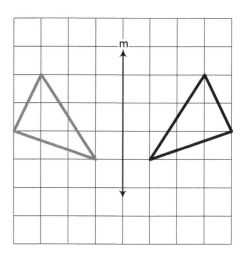

(b)

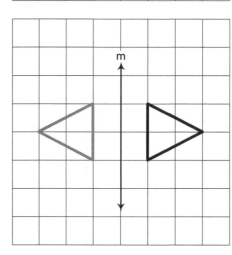

(e)

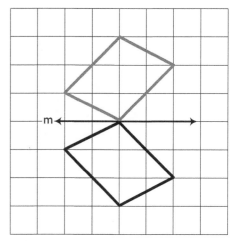

(c)

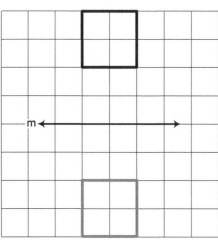

(f)

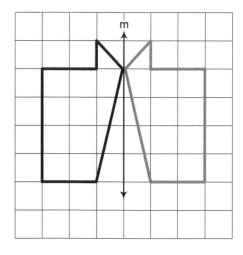

2. (a)

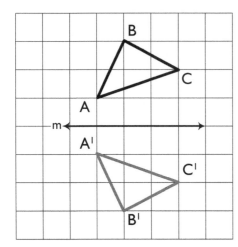

(b)

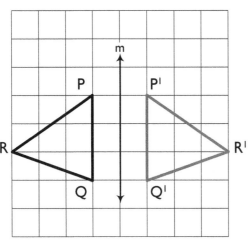

(c)

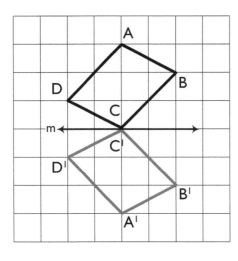

(d)

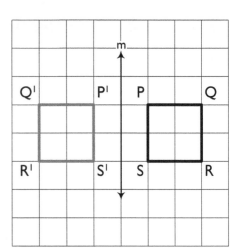

(e)

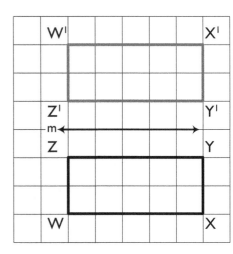

(f)

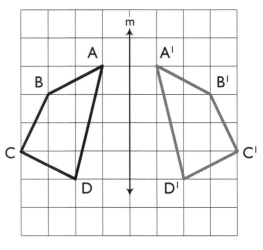

3. (a)

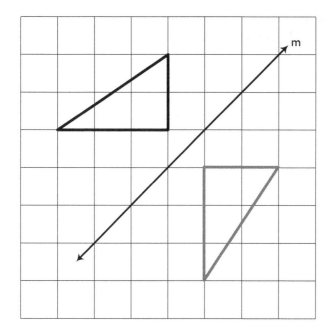

(b)

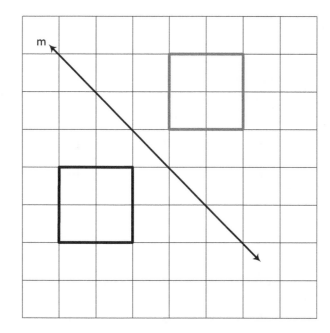

End of chapter activity: Reflection by design

Check pupils' designs.

Chapter 24: 3D shapes

Exercise 24.1 : 3D shapes

1.

	Name of shape	Shape(s) of faces	Number of faces	Number of corners	Number of edges
(i)	Cube	Square	6	8	12
(ii)	Cuboid	Rectangle	6	8	12
(iii)	Pyramid (triangle base)	Triangle (usually equilateral)	4	4	6
(iv)	Pyramid (square base)	Isosceles triangle Square	5	5	8
(v)	Triangular prism	Triangle Rectangle	5	6	9

2. (a)

	Number of faces (F)	Number of corners (C)	Faces and corners (F+C)	Number of edges (E)
Cube	6	8	14	12
Cuboid	6	8	14	12
Pyramid (triangle base)	4	4	8	6
Pyramid (square base)	5	5	10	8
Triangular prism	5	6	11	9

(b) F + C is 2 more than E

(c) (i) 15 (ii) 9 (iii) 20

3. (a)

	Faces	Corners	Edges
(i)	7	10	15
(ii)	8	12	18

(b) (i) Number of faces is 2 more than the number of sides of cross section

(ii) Number of edges is 3 times the number of sides of cross section

(c) Yes. F + C = E + 2

(d) Both have a regular cross-section

End of chapter activity: Monkey business

Down at A
$A \rightarrow F \rightarrow E \rightarrow H$
$A \rightarrow F \rightarrow G \rightarrow H$
$A \rightarrow B \rightarrow C \rightarrow D \rightarrow A \rightarrow F \rightarrow E \rightarrow H$
$A \rightarrow B \rightarrow C \rightarrow D \rightarrow A \rightarrow F \rightarrow G \rightarrow H$
$A \rightarrow D \rightarrow C \rightarrow B \rightarrow A \rightarrow F \rightarrow E \rightarrow H$
$A \rightarrow D \rightarrow C \rightarrow B \rightarrow A \rightarrow F \rightarrow G \rightarrow H$

Down at B
$A \rightarrow B \rightarrow G \rightarrow H$
$A \rightarrow B \rightarrow G \rightarrow F \rightarrow E \rightarrow H$
$A \rightarrow D \rightarrow C \rightarrow B \rightarrow G \rightarrow H$
$A \rightarrow D \rightarrow C \rightarrow B \rightarrow G \rightarrow F \rightarrow E \rightarrow H$

Down at C
$A \rightarrow B \rightarrow C \rightarrow H$
$A \rightarrow D \rightarrow C \rightarrow H$

Down at D
$A \rightarrow D \rightarrow E \rightarrow H$
$A \rightarrow D \rightarrow E \rightarrow F \rightarrow G \rightarrow H$
$A \rightarrow B \rightarrow C \rightarrow D \rightarrow E \rightarrow H$
$A \rightarrow B \rightarrow C \rightarrow D \rightarrow E \rightarrow F \rightarrow G \rightarrow H$

Shortest route   30 m

Longest route   70 m

Chapter 25: Perimeter and area

Exercise 25.1: Perimeter

1. (a) 16 cm
   (b) 20 cm
   (c) 20 cm
   (d) 28 cm

2. (a) 26 cm
   (b) 50 cm
   (c) 80 cm
   (d) 20.8 cm
   (e) 40 cm

3. (a) 36 cm
   (b) 64 cm
   (c) 80 cm
   (d) 18 cm
   (e) 28.8 cm
   (f) 26.4 cm

Exercise 25.2: Calculating length and width

1. (a) 4 cm
   (b) 3 cm
   (c) 20 cm
   (d) 16 cm
   (e) 1.5 cm

2. (a) 4 cm
   (b) 16 cm
   (c) 25 cm

Exercise 25.3: Area

1. 15 cm²
2. 24 cm²
3. 9 cm²
4. 25 cm²
5. 16 cm²
6. 26 cm²
7. 24 cm²
8. 18 cm²
9. 13.5 cm²
10. 20 cm²
11. 15 cm²
12. 10 cm²
13. 8 cm²
14. 18 cm²
15. 63 cm²

Exercise 25.4: Summary exercise

1. 28 cm
2. 28 cm
3. 15 cm
4. 15 cm
5. 8 cm
6. 6 cm

7. (a) 24 cm²
   (b) 16 cm²
   (c) 18 cm²
   (d) 22.5 cm²

End of chapter activity: Same perimeter, different area

11 cm x 1 cm → 11 cm²

10 cm x 2 cm → 20 cm²

9 cm x 3 cm → 27 cm²

8 cm x 4 cm → 32 cm²

7 cm x 5 cm → 35 cm²

6 cm x 6 cm → 36 cm²

The square gives the larges area (36 cm²)

The largest area that can be enclosed by a quadrilateral whose perimeter is 40 cm is 100 cm² (a square of side 10 cm)

Chapter 26: Mental strategies

Exercise 26.1: Using addition strategies

1.	98	9.	176	17.	209	25.	580
2.	79	10.	169	18.	923	26.	598
3.	81	11.	142	19.	684	27.	602
4.	58	12.	112	20.	967	28.	752
5.	123	13.	170	21.	452	29.	600
6.	148	14.	156	22.	728	30.	902
7.	132	15.	92	23.	817		
8.	164	16.	312	24.	379		

Exercise 26.2: Doubling

1.	110	6.	161	11.	360	16.	550
2.	170	7.	176	12.	420	17.	920
3.	140	8.	134	13.	385	18.	730
4.	142	9.	53	14.	430	19.	756
5.	123	10.	145	15.	780	20.	1000

Exercise 26.3: Addition using a number line

1.	181	9.	156	17.	870	25.	170
2.	105	10.	163	18.	914	26.	600
3.	121	11.	246	19.	964	27.	272
4.	175	12.	574	20.	982	28.	898
5.	85	13.	342	21.	161	29.	950
6.	83	14.	430	22.	209	30.	825
7.	152	15.	729	23.	165		
8.	111	16.	900	24.	184		

Exercise 26.4: Subtracting by 'counting on'

1.	4	6.	5	11.	5	16.	7
2.	5	7.	5	12.	6	17.	9
3.	7	8.	5	13.	5	18.	9
4.	6	9.	7	14.	4	19.	8
5.	7	10.	11	15.	8	20.	7

Exercise 26.5: Subtraction with a number line (1)

1.	21	6.	46	11.	79	16.	232
2.	28	7.	44	12.	86	17.	185
3.	44	8.	78	13.	108	18.	252
4.	47	9.	117	14.	218	19.	183
5.	36	10.	151	15.	164	20.	511

Exercise 26.6: Subtracting by 'counting back'

1.	6	6.	8	11.	6	16.	12
2.	7	7.	8	12.	9	17.	14
3.	7	8.	11	13.	9	18.	9
4.	9	9.	7	14.	7	19.	8
5.	4	10.	9	15.	6	20.	8

Exercise 26.7: Subtraction with a number line (2)

1.	24	6.	32	11.	64	16.	26
2.	25	7.	25	12.	88	17.	73
3.	15	8.	21	13.	286	18.	445
4.	36	9.	24	14.	276	19.	397
5.	27	10.	33	15.	387	20.	504

Exercise 26.8: Multiplication by partition

1.	96	6.	280	11.	288	16.	1024
2.	102	7.	161	12.	966	17.	1462
3.	108	8.	153	13.	875	18.	1311
4.	315	9.	230	14.	928	19.	1178
5.	108	10.	348	15.	972	20.	2756

Exercise 26.9: Multiplying using factors

1.	216	6.	416	11.	2205	16.	966
2.	360	7.	912	12.	1325	17.	2220
3.	1050	8.	2240	13.	1494	18.	3456
4.	1080	9.	555	14.	1608	19.	1944
5.	308	10.	2016	15.	1520	20.	1512

Exercise 26.10: Multiplying using doubling

1. 156
2. 138
3. (a) (i) 45
       (ii) 90
       (iii) 180
       (iv) 360
       (v) 720
   (b) (i) 540
       (ii) 855

4. 1080
5. 1440
6. 1395
7. 1575

Exercise 26.11: Division

1. 7
2. 45
3. 6
4. 70
5. 12
6. 22
7. 48
8. 45
9. 39
10. 25
11. 19
12. 33
13. 25
14. 16
15. 52
16. 47
17. 30
18. 50
19. 46
20. 16
21. 19
22. 14
23. 15
24. 14
25. 17
26. 54
27. 32
28. 37
29. 57
30. 43

Designer Anne Wilson
Editor Diana Loxley

Picture Editor Anne Fraser
Picture Research Sue Gladstone
Production Nicky Bowden

AUTHORS' ACKNOWLEDGMENTS
We would like to thank all the people who opened their houses to us and whose lives we disturbed, including Chris Coppack, Belinda Hextall and Vanessa Rhodes. Many thanks to Lady Davina Gibbs, Barry McNamara, Helena Mercer, Graham Piggot and Andrew Townsend for providing additional information and contacts and to all the people on Annie Sloan's courses who have contributed their thoughts. Indeed, the happy connections we have made have often led to the most interesting, fresh ideas. Also thanks to Claire Ansell and Kris Grainger for their help and to Saskia and Kit Smith and Hugo, Henry and Thomas (Felix) Manuel for their patience.

PUBLISHER'S ACKNOWLEDGMENTS
The publishers would like to thank the following individuals and companies for their help in producing this book: Sallie Coolidge, Penny David and Matthew Sturgis for their editorial contributions, Katy Foskew for her excellent clerical work and Niki Medlikova for design assistance; Patrick Baty and John Sutcliffe for their valuable advice; Valerie Bingham and Susanne Haines for initial editorial work; Ian Bristow for information on the use of colour in historic houses; Carol Dethloff for picture research; William Gallagher, Curator, St Columb's and the Glebe Gallery, County Donegal; Tom Helme for historical guidance; Potmolen Paint of Warminster for their help with 'Special Paints & Finishes'; Smallbone of Devizes for allowing us to use their photographs of Peter Sheppard's house; Stephen L. Wolf for his help and advice. We are grateful to everyone who allowed their houses to be photographed: Susy Benn, David Hicks, the proprietors of 'Muthaiga', Adeline Nolan, Merlin Pennink and Annie Sloan.

PHOTOGRAPHIC ACKNOWLEDGMENTS
(A = above   AL = above left   AR = above right   B = below
BL = below left   BR = below right   L = left   R = right)

Agence Top/Pascal Chevalier: 48, 115L, 147; Roland Beaufre: 149;
Peter Aprahamian: 23, 46A
Arcaid/Richard Bryant: 6, 17, 52, 79R, 83R, 88, 94B, 102L, 108, 110, 112, 113R, 115R, 120R, 135BL, 153A, 157B, 160A, 165AR; Jeremy Cockayne: 81R; Mark Fiennes: 77R; Lucinda Lambton: 34B, 85, 102R, 120L; Alberto Piovano: 79L
Arc Studios/Sue Atkinson © FLL: 40L, 65R, 90R, 103R, 176–185
Laura Ashley: 159AR
Auro Organic Paints (GB) Ltd: 174
Art Directors Photo Library/Larry Lee: 153BL
Paul Barker: 50, 122/23, 141R
Oliver Benn: 131A, 136L
Boys Syndication/Michael Boys: 26R, 34A, 58R, 116A, 118B
Camera Press: 15R, 124; Peo Eriksson: 13, 64, 95, 113L, 161AL; Brunno Müller: 27
Geoff Dann © FLL: 100/01
Michael Dunne © FLL: 164R
Elle Decoration/Transworld: 57L, 83L
John Freeman: 14B

Karl-Erik Granath: 32, 40R, 47R
John Hall: 14A, 25, 91, 118A, 129
Lars Hallen: front cover, 45, 67, 80, 86R, 114A, 157AL, 158R
Lizzie Himmel: 35, 63L, 70R, 72, 109B, 139R
Ian Howes © FLL: 12L, 33L, 51R, 78R, 99AR, 136R, 153BR, 167BL
Jacqui Hurst © FLL: 20/21
Ken Kirkwood: 96, 105L
Andrew Lawson: 42/3
Barbara Lloyd: 77L, 152L, 169L
Norman McGrath: 82AR
John Miller: 55B
Derry Moore: 1, 16R, 24, 28, 39L, 71, 76, 167AL
James Mortimer: back cover, 36, 37L, 66; courtesy of Smallbone: 31, 33R, 138, 139L, 141L
David Murray © FLL: 61L, 65L, 105R, 116B, 132L, 135A
Jean-Bernard Naudin: 22
Hugh Palmer: 117
Julie Phipps: 57R
Ianthe Ruthven: 2, 15L, 39R, 41, 46B, 49, 54B, 55A, 63R, 73AL, 84, 87, 93R, 103L, 114B, 119, 128A, 150, 154R, 159BR, 165B; © FLL: 12R, 18, 38, 53, 61R, 70L, 81L, 98, 99BL, 106, 107L, 109A, 170BR
Paul Ryan/J.B. Visual Press: 94A, 126, 137, 145A, 152R
Fritz von der Schulenburg: 54A, 58L, 59, 62, 68, 69, 73B, 82AL, 82B, 86L, 89L, 90L, 92, 97, 99AL, 107R, 111L, 121, 130, 131B, 132R, 134, 135BR, 140, 143, 144B, 145BL, 146, 148, 157AR
Marc Stanes: 51L
Jay Whitcombe: 104
Elizabeth Whiting & Associates/Tim Street-Porter: 10, 11, 16L, 56R, 74/75, 78L, 168; Peter Wolosynski: 125A, 145BR
The World of *Interiors*/Tim Beddow: 30A; Nadia MacKenzie: 133
World Press Network Ltd/IPC Magazines: 26L, 29, 30B, 37R, 44L, 60, 93L, 111R, 125B, 127, 128B, 142R

For permission to reproduce the drawings, paintings and photographs in this book, the Publishers thank:
Bibliothèque Forney, Paris: 160B
Bracken Books, London: 47L, 162AL, 167R
The British Museum, London (By Courtesy of the Trustees): 44A, 56L, 155BL, 155R
The Design Museum, London: 170L
Fine Art Photographs and Library Ltd: 163
Laing Art Gallery, Newcastle Upon Tyne (By Courtesy of Tyne and Wear Museums Service): 166A
Mary Evans Picture Library: 159L
Musée d'Art et d'Histoire, Geneva: 144A
The National Gallery, London (By Courtesy of the Trustees): 154L, 155A
Royal Academy of Arts, London: 158L
Sir John Soane's Museum, London (By Courtesy of the Trustees): 161BL
The Tate Gallery, London: 142L
Victoria & Albert Museum, London (By Courtesy of the Board of Trustees): 89R, 156R, 161R, 162R, 164L, 165AL, 166B, 169AR, 170AR
The Wallace Collection, London (reproduced by kind permission of the Trustees): 156L
Yale University Art and Architecture Library: Birren Collection of Books on Color: 19, 151, 171